TH'OWXIYA

TH'OWXIYA
THE HUNGRY FEAST DISH
BY JOSEPH A. DANDURAND

PLAYWRIGHTS CANADA PRESS
TORONTO

For professional or amateur production rights, please contact:
Axis Theatre Company
1405 Anderson Street, Granville Island, Vancouver, BC V6H 3R5
www.axistheatre.com :: tours@axistheatre.com :: 604.669.0631 :: 1.866.294.7943

LIBRARY AND ARCHIVES CANADA CATALOGUING IN PUBLICATION
Title: Th'owxiya : the hungry feast dish / by Joseph A. Dandurand.
Names: Dandurand, Joseph A., author.
Description: First edition. | A play.
Identifiers: Canadiana (print) 20190149000 | Canadiana (ebook) 20190149019 |
ISBN 9780369100238 (softcover) | ISBN 9780369100245 (PDF)
| ISBN 9780369100252 (EPUB) | ISBN 9780369100269 (Kindle)
Classification: LCC PS8557.A523 T46 2019 | DDC jC812/.54—dc23

Playwrights Canada Press acknowledges that we operate on land, which, for thousands of years, has been the traditional territories of the Mississaugas of the Credit, Huron-Wendat, Anishinaabe, Métis, and Haudenosaunee peoples. Today, this meeting place is home to many Indigenous peoples from across Turtle Island and we are grateful to have the opportunity to work and play here.

We acknowledge the financial support of the Canada Council for the Arts— which last year invested $153 million to bring the arts to Canadians throughout the country—the Ontario Arts Council (OAC), Ontario Creates, and the Government of Canada for our publishing activities.

Canada Council for the Arts   Conseil des arts du Canada

ONTARIO ARTS COUNCIL
CONSEIL DES ARTS DE L'ONTARIO
an Ontario government agency
un organisme du gouvernement de l'Ontario

Canada

ONTARIO CREATES | ONTARIO CRÉATIF

To my mother,
Josette Audrey Dandurand,
a true survivor.

Th'owxiya: The Hungry Feast Dish was first produced by Axis Theatre from June 20 to July 1, 2017, at the UBC Botanical Gardens with the following cast and creative team:

Merewyn Comeau: Percussionist / Th'owxiya
Braiden Houle: Kw'at'el (Mouse)
Chelsea Rose: Sasq'ets (Sasquatch)
Taran Kootenhayoo: Sqeweqs (Raven)
Tai Grauman: Girl Theqa:t (Tree) / Girl Spa:th (Bear)
Mitchell Saddleback: Boy Theqa:t (Tree) / Boy Spa:th (Bear)

Director / Dramaturg: Chris McGregor
Set, Prop, Costume and Mask Designer: Jay Havens
Composer and Musical Director: Marguerite Witvoet
Sound Designer: Stephen Bulat
Movement Coach: Nyla Carpentier
Stage Manager: Madison Henry
Apprentice Stage Manager: Jessica Keenan
Assistant Concept Design: Carrielynn Victor
Production Manager / Builder: Stephen Beaver
Assistant to the Director / Puppet Advisor / Puppet Builder: Mika Laulainen
Advisor to the Production: Deneh'Cho Thompson
Feast Dish Carvers: Earl Moulton and Don Froese

Cedar Hats Builder: Gracie Kelly
Regalia: Darlene Harris
Stitching: Tracy Wright and Jay Havens
Set Painting: Jay Havens and Kelly Oberholtzer; Aaron El Sabrout, Matt G.F. McLean
Puppets: Jay Havens, Mika Laulainan, and cast of *Th'owxiya*

CHARACTERS

Th'owxiya [Tho-wox-eeya]: A feast dish that lies on her back and has a large open mouth. In the spirit world she is a cannibal woman, a basket ogress who likes the taste of children and any other foods found in the spirit world. She can be played as a voice recording or by an actor.

Storytellers / Syuwe [Soo-way]: Like a Greek chorus. Each character plays the role of a storyteller. They introduce each scene and change the spindle whorl as the story moves forwards. They are played by all five actors.

Sasq'ets [Sass-kets] (Sasquatch): A servant for Th'owxiya. A sasquatch who has become bored with the duties that it takes to care for Th'owxiya, and who may at any time be eaten by her. Played by Actor 1.

Kw'at'el [Kwa-ot-tel] (Mouse): A very quick and skittish mouse who likes cheese and chasing his tail. Played by Actor 2.

Sqeweqs [Skway-ex] (Raven): A very sly and cool raven. Played by Actor 3.

3

Girl Theqa:t [Thay-ket] (Tree) / **Girl Spa:th [Spa-ath]** (Bear) and
Boy Theqa:t / Boy Spa:th: Two young trees / bears. As they enter
the spirit world they appear as young, frightened trees who have
lost their parents. They soon realize they must become young bears
in order to face the many challenges of survival in the spirit world.
Played by Actors 4 and 5.

SETTING

Prop food in baskets is given to the kids in the front row prior to
the start of the show so that Sasq'ets can gather them from the
"people" as offerings to place in and around the feast dish. The
entire play takes place within the Kwantlen village of Squa'lets,
which means "where waters divide." All of the action takes place
in front of a traditional Kwantlen plank house with a door-mouth
opening. In our case, this is the Spirit World. The other side of the
door-mouth is the Real World.

Th'owxiya sits centre stage of the village. The voice of Th'owxiya can
be projected through speakers around the stage. Character masks
spread out about the stage on boxes and in baskets with drums.

INTRODUCTION STORYTELLING

Drumming.

Through a "Welcome Song" the five storytellers enter from off stage.

The song ends.

ACTOR 1: I am a Storyteller

ACTOR 2: I am a Storyteller

ACTOR 3: I am a Storyteller

ACTOR 4 & ACTOR 5: And I am a Storyteller

ALL: This story . . .

ACTOR 1: . . . Is from the Kwantlen people

ACTOR 1 makes a "welcome" hand gesture.

They once lived in the sky
And were known
As sky people

ACTOR 2: But one day they came
Down to earth
When the great Sun
Came to them
And told them
To take the salmon
From the river

ACTOR 3: The Kwantlen people
Believe
In the spirit power
They believe
In the power of
The animals

ACTOR 1: The birds

ACTOR 2: Rocks

ACTOR 4: Trees

ACTOR 5: Fish

ACTOR 3: and even
The power of
A spindle whorl

The ACTORS stop and show the audience the spindle whorl.

ACTOR 4: This is a spindle

ACTOR 3: And this is a spindle whorl

ACTOR 4: They have not been used
For generations
But now they can tell stories
Look at them
Aren't they beautiful?

ACTOR 3: Which one shall we choose?
This one? Yes good choice . . .

ACTOR 4: If you look closely
You can see
Beautiful shapes
That have been
Painted and carved
Into the whorl

ACTOR 5: The Kwantlen
Are great believers
In the world
They cannot see
And so we tell stories
So that we can be
At peace with the spirits

ACTOR 3: Each whorl in this tale
Will tell a story
About a wonderful spirit

ACTOR 2: This whorl will
Tell us a tale
About a great feast

ACTOR 3: I place the whorl
And we begin this tale

> *ACTOR 4 begins to spin the spindle as the beat quickens.*

ACTOR 4: We must tell you
This tale
Before the whorl
Becomes too hot

> *ACTOR 1 puts on a mask: SASQ'ETS begins to move. She pre-*
> *pares the food for the feast. She moves very quickly, gathering*
> *food from the kids in the audience as she avoids the mouth of*
> *TH'OWXIYA. TH'OWXIYA begins to laugh. Thunder comes crash-*
> *ing down as SASQ'ETS freezes and stares at the sky.*

SASQ'ETS: *(to audience)* Isn't she beautiful?
This wondrous dish

> *Drumming. She goes back to work.*

ACTOR 4: Let us watch
As the Sasquatch—Sasq'ets—prepares
Food for her

These foods
Are gifts
From the many
People of this earth

TH'OWXIYA WHORL

ACTOR 4: Th'owxiya was taken from the great forest
Now she rests here in the spirit world for all to see
Such beauty in her eyes and mouth

SASQ'ETS: But beware!
Beware of her mouth
For she likes the taste of humans

Beware!
She likes to eat children
Beware of her mouth!

Yes, Th'owxiya is always hungry
The great Th'owxiya can get very angry
I must prepare a feast
I must prepare a feast or else
I must prepare a feast
Or else
She will eat me!

Yes, she will eat me!
The great Th'owxiya will dine upon me
We do not want that
No, I do not want to be eaten
I must prepare the feast
Or, she will eat me!

I do not want to be eaten!
Do you want to be eaten? . . . No I didn't think so
Have you seen Th'owxiya eat?
She has giant teeth and she spits fire!
And she burned my backside!

There must be food for Th'owxiya to eat!
If not, she will not sleep
She will not sleep

She will not sleep
She will not sleep

She must have tasty foods
I must prepare them
She likes them warm
She likes them tasty

> SASQ'ETS *finishes her work around* TH'OWXIYA *and moves off stage to watch with the others.* KW'AT'EL *enters through the house.*

KW'AT'EL: The spirit world!

KW'AT'EL goes to the large whorl on the floor stage right and looks at the painted images.

Look at the beautiful pictures. They are the spirits of the Kwantlen people. There is a sun, two moons, the Raven, two Spirit Bears, and two Salmon. In the Kwantlen language, Raven is Sqeweqs, Bear is Spa:th and Salmon is Stheqi. These spirits shall help me in my journey for food. Oh, and I am Kw'at'el. Can you guess what I am?

KIDS: Turkey? Rat? Fox? Mouse?

KW'AT'EL: . . . Right! Mouse!

I am so hungry. In my world, food is very hard to come by, but the spirit world has wonderful foods. The ancestors say there is a Great Spirit by the name of Th'owxiya. Some ancestors say she is a cannibal, which means she likes to eat people. Mostly she likes to eat children.

The ancestors also say that Th'owxiya keeps tasty foods from all parts of the earth inside her belly and her mouth. If you are sly enough, the ancestors say you can borrow food from her. I am Kw'at'el and I am not afraid of this Th'owxiya.

This cannibal woman. This basket ogress of the spirit world. Oh, I am sooo hungry. Let me show you how I "borrow" food from the great Th'owxiya.

KW'AT'EL scurries towards TH'OWXIYA. As KW'AT'EL gets closer to her, he slows down and begins to creep ever so closer to her mouth, where a tasty piece of cheese is . . . KW'AT'EL inches

*closer, then reaches ever so slowly into her mouth and pulls
out a piece of cheese. Just as he stuffs the piece of cheese into his
mouth,* SASQ'ETS *begins to move frantically. She runs around*
TH'OWXIYA *trying to figure out what has happened and which
piece of food is missing. Thunder is heard and* TH'OWXIYA
begins to laugh and then speak.

TH'OWXIYA: I smell Kw'at'el. Is that you, Kw'at'el?

KW'AT'EL does not move. SASQ'ETS *comes up behind him and he
begins to sniff him.* KW'AT'EL *just stands there with his mouth
stuffed with cheese.*

It is you, Kw'at'el. My eyes are not what they used to be. Sasq'ets is
tired and lazy. She does not protect my food the way she used to. If
she is not careful one day I may eat her for dessert. Now, Kw'at'el,
why do you steal food from my mouth?

KW'AT'EL speaks with the cheese still stuffed in his mouth.

KW'AT'EL: What food? There is *nothing* in my mouth.

TH'OWXIYA: Not anymore. Sasq'ets, take the cheese out of his
mouth and put it back into mine.

*SASQ'ETS takes the cheese from KW'AT'EL's mouth and puts it
back into TH'OWXIYA's, but not before taking a small piece for
herself.*

Now, Kw'at'el, you know the penalty for stealing food from my
mouth. Anyone caught stealing food from my mouth shall be eaten

along with all of their family. Sasq'ets, prepare Kw'at'el and gather his family so I may eat them, too!

KW'AT'EL: But surely I can repay you for my little mistake. Name it and I shall do it!

TH'OWXIYA: Ummmm . . . for you and your family not to be eaten, you would need to bring to me two *children* that I could eat. If you do not bring me two children by the time the second moon rises above the great mountain, then I shall eat you and your family with a nice . . . sauce . . . prepared for me by Sasq'ets. It has been a long time since I've eaten Kw'at'el for dinner. Do not think that I will not have my wish! Kw'at'el, you have until the second moon rises above the great mountain to find me two children. Go now!!

Thunder is heard as TH'OWXIYA laughs. SASQ'ETS dances around KW'AT'EL as the laughter and thunder fade away.

KW'AT'EL: Ohh, What must I do? . . . Ahhhhh!

He chases his tail then stops.

I do not know of any children in the spirit world. Where would I find children?

SASQ'ETS: You must look in the forest
You must go to the trees
They say the forest hides children
Yes, this is what they say

They say the forest is full
Yes, it is full with children
These children are the trees
Yes, this is what they say

KW'AT'EL: I have no time to go to the forest. I must get back and protect my family.

SASQ'ETS: Th'owxiya has sent for your family
She will have them
She will have them for dinner

You have until the second moon rises
You have until the second moon touches the night
And rises above the great mountain
Go, Kw'at'el!
Go to the forest
There you will find trees
And these trees *are* the children

KW'AT'EL: I am going back to my house. MY children need me to protect them. I am not afraid of Th'owxiya!

> *Thunder.* KW'AT'EL *jumps and scurries to his house, looks back one last time and then exits.*

SASQ'ETS: I must prepare the sauce
Yes, the sauce
I almost forgot!
Get the sauce ready
Get it ready or else
Or else I will be the sauce!

TH'OWXIYA's laughter is heard as the sound of thunder begins to rumble. ACTOR 3 stops spinning the spindle and changes the whorl.

FOREST WHORL

ACTOR 2: Now we must change the whorl

ACTOR 3: This whorl shall
Tell us the next
Part of this story

ACTOR 2: This is the part about the forest
The forest is so wonderful
And powerful

Even Th'owxiya
Was taken from this forest

ACTOR 3: Isn't she beautiful
This wondrous dish
She was taken
From the great forest

ACTOR 1: And now she rests here
In the spirit world
For all to see

ACTOR 3: Now we must learn
About the forest
And her beautiful children

ACTOR 2: The trees used to be
So happy and filled with life
But now they cry
They are lost and alone
And they search
For their parents
Who have been taken

ACTOR 3: Taken away
Away

ACTOR 1: We spin this tale
So you may learn
And remember
Why the forests of the world
Have become empty
And lonely

> *A young GIRL THEQA:T (tree) and a BOY THEQA:T appear*
> *through the door-mouth of their house. They enter and walk*
> *downstage as SASQ'ETS freezes. A chainsaw can be heard in the*
> *distance, softly but audible.*

GIRL THEQA:T: Brother, where are we?

BOY THEQA:T: The spirit world . . .

GIRL THEQA:T: But why are we . . .

The chainsaw grows louder.

. . . What is that noise?

BOY THEQA:T: Our parents are falling.

GIRL THEQA:T: Why do they fall?

BOY THEQA:T: So people may write upon us.

GIRL THEQA:T: What do they write?

BOY THEQA:T: They write that we were once great and tall.

The chainsaw grows even louder then fades out completely.

GIRL THEQA:T: Will they come for us?

BOY THEQA:T: They will come *only* when we are great and tall.

GIRL THEQA:T: Where do they take our parents?

BOY THEQA:T: I do not know.

GIRL THEQA:T: We must find them. They will be lonely without us. We must find them.

BOY THEQA:T: Yes . . .

GIRL THEQA:T: What shall we do?

BOY THEQA:T: We must change ourselves.

GIRL THEQA:T: What shall we become?

BOY THEQA:T: We shall become Spa:th.

GIRL THEQA:T: How do we become Spa:th?

SASQ'ETS pulls out an apple and gives it to the GIRL THEQA:T.

BOY THEQA:T: We must eat the apples in this spirit world.

He takes a bite. She takes a bite.

GIRL THEQA:T: How sweet it tastes.

BOY THEQA:T: Yes, full of life.

GIRL THEQA:T: I am becoming Spa:th.

BOY THEQA:T: I too am becoming Spa:th.

The BOY THEQA:T gives the apple back to SASQ'ETS, who again steals a bite before putting it back into the eye of TH'OWXIYA. SASQ'ETS freezes as the BOY THEQA:T and the GIRL THEQA:T slowly take off their tree costumes or the other ACTORS help them transform. They both go upstage and hang their tree costumes off stage on either side of the door-mouth. ACTOR 2 begins.

SQEWEQS WHORL

ACTOR 2: They have just become Spa:th
And now they
Begin their journey

We must again
Change the whorl

ACTOR 3: I will choose the
Sqeweqs whorl

ACTOR 2: The Sqeweqs shall
Teach the Spa:th
How to gather food

ACTOR 1: Yes this is a good story
Yes this is a good tale

> *ACTOR 2 changes the whorl and begins to spin the spindle as
> the BOY SPA:TH and the GIRL SPA:TH sit and hold their empty
> bellies.*

BOY SPA:TH: We need Sqeweqs!

GIRL SPA:TH: Yes, we need Sqeweqs to help us hunt for food!

They both call out for SQEWEQS. SQEWEQS appears through the door-mouth. He's tired, grumpy and his belly is also empty.

BOY SPA:TH & GIRL SPA:TH: Sqeweqs! Sqeweqs!! Sqeweqs!!!

SQEWEQS: CAA CAA. Who dares to call me from my sleep? There are no FAT worms to be eaten in the *morning*, only skinny, yucky ones. Why do you wake me?

GIRL SPA:TH: We need to find food. Our bellies are empty and we do not know what food to eat.

BOY SPA:TH: We need to find food. You are Sqeweqs, aren't you?

SQEWEQS: I am the Sqeweqs. CAA CAA.

GIRL SPA:TH: How do we gather food? Do Spa:th eat worms?

BOY SPA:TH: Yes, I am so hungry. I could eat a worm.

The BOY SPA:TH begins to look for worms. SQEWEQS laughs at him.

SQEWEQS: Spa:th. Spa:th. Spa:th are big and strong. CAA CAA. Spa:th eat salmon from the raging rivers. Spa:th eat berries. Spa:th eat Kw'at'el, Spa:th eat, hey . . . Spa:th eat everything!

The BOY SPA:TH finds a fat worm. He stares at it, not knowing what to do with it.

BOY SPA:TH: Look! I've found a fat worm.

GIRL SPA:TH: Let me see! Let me see!

SQEWEQS: Let me see that worm! I must inspect all worms in this world.

SQEWEQS takes the worm, sniffs it, holds it above his beak and then swallows it whole.

Yep, that's a good worm.

BOY SPA:TH: That was my worm!

He chases SQEWEQS.

SQEWEQS: You must learn the proper way to catch and then eat worms.

The GIRL SPA:TH finds a worm.

GIRL SPA:TH: I've found one! I've found one!

SQEWEQS: Let me see it! I must inspect each and every worm of this world.

The GIRL SPA:TH holds it up and teases SQEWEQS with it. She then repeats SQEWEQS's method of eating worms.

She learns fast this young Spa:th.

The GIRL SPA:TH burps.

Come, let me teach you the proper way to catch and eat worms.

All three continue to look for worms. They eat and laugh. They become full and sleepy. The BOY SPA:TH and GIRL SPA:TH curl up together and SQEWEQS sleeps upstage.

WINGS WHORL

ACTOR 1: I love that Sqeweqs
He really is
A kind spirit

ACTOR 2: Those young Spa:th
Will learn many lessons
From Sqeweqs
And they will be able
To find their parents

Thunder.

ACTOR 1: I hear thunder

ACTOR 2: Yes the Spa:th
Must learn
About the thunder

ACTOR 1: But first
Sqeweqs will teach
Them how to fly

ACTOR 2: Yes and they will learn
About the thunder
And about the earth
And how it is disappearing

ACTOR 1: They must learn
How to eat from the earth
But they must also learn
How to give back
What they have taken
Yes this is a good lesson
Yes this is a good story

> *ACTOR 1 spins the spindle whorl. SASQ'ETS dances around*
> *TH'OWXIYA. The drum grows louder and then stops. SASQ'ETS*
> *stops. SQEWEQS wakes up from his comfortable sleep . . .*
> *yawning.*

SQEWEQS: CAA CAA . . .

> *SQEWEQS pulls out a spoon and begins to carve it with his*
> *talons.*

Look at those Spa:th. Spa:th sleep forever. Snug *as a* bug. CAA. I am
Sqeweqs and I choose to watch and laugh at the world. CAA. I laugh
at the world. CAA, CAA. I laugh at the world.

> *He puts away his spoon.*

You've heard me as I fly away to the warm sun. The warm sun. I
think I shall fly away right now and touch the warm sun.

He begins to flap his wings. The BOY SPA:TH *and the* GIRL
SPA:TH *wake up and begin to stretch.*

We shall teach the Spa:th how to fly. We will show them the earth.
First you must flap your wings . . .

They hold up their arms.

. . . Well then flap your furry arms then. You must allow the wind
to guide and help you. Up we go. Can you guys fly?

(to audience) Come on, flap your arms and imagine that you are
great birds. I am Sqeweqs.

SQEWEQS *flies, pulling children up.*

You must be another bird, there is only one Sqeweqs. Who are you?
Are you an eagle—Sp'oq'es? Owl—Chitmexw?

SQEWEQS *flies with the children in a circle.*

Come with me to the warm sun.

SQEWEQS, *the* BOY SPA:TH *and the* GIRL SPA:TH *fly around*
TH'OWXIYA. *The kids from the audience join.*

I touched the sun. Did you guys touch the sun? Wasn't it wonderful? We should fly to the moon. When the night comes we will fly
and touch the moon, but now my wings are tired. Are your wings
tired? Flying is so exhausting. We must eat more worms. Do you
have any more worms? Well, what should we do? Should we steal

the sun and eat it? No, too hot! Should we eat the moon? No, too cold! Should we eat the earth? . . .

SQEWEQS pulls out his spoon.

. . . Yes, but we must not eat too much. We must save some for the next generation. Remember that, do not eat too much of the earth. Save some. Save some for me and my big belly . . . Ohh, I am hungry . . .

He puts his spoon away.

. . . CAA CAA I saw some berries. I remember seeing some berries . . . Did you guys see some delicious berries? Where?

KIDS: There! There!

SQEWEQS goes to a basket of berries left out in front of TH'OWXIYA by SASQ'ETS some time ago.

SQEWEQS: Thank you! Look, someone has left some berries for us to eat.

SQEWEQS sits in front of TH'OWXIYA and begins to eat all the berries. He forgets about the SPA:TH and is only concerned with filling his belly.

GIRL SPA:TH: What about us?

BOY SPA:TH: Yeah, we want some of those sweet berries too!

SQEWEQS looks up from his berries. He realizes that everyone is staring at him and that they hunger for his berries.

SQEWEQS: Of course. Never let it be said that Sqeweqs would not share his berries . . . well, someone else's berries anyway.

The SPA:TH eat the berries. SQEWEQS perches on a box.

SQEWEQS: Ahh! Spa:th! Flying to the sun takes its toll on an old Sqeweqs like me. I must rest and enjoy the hot sun. The first moon will be out soon and we can fly to it. So get your beautiful bird wings ready because the next time we will fly, it will be to the moon. But now, I must rest. These wings are not what they used to be. Must sleep. Must sleep *and* dream . . . these young Spa:th need to learn how to fish for Stheqi. I will show them . . . with a little help.

SQEWEQS yawns.

. . . CAA CAA . . . See you later, my beautiful friends. See you later, my feathered friends. See you by the light of the moon. CAA!

SQEWEQS sleeps. The BOY SPA:TH and the GIRL SPA:TH continue to eat all the berries they can find. They begin to play and look for more berries, but there are none left. They play some more. The sun slowly sinks and disappears as the moon slowly rises. SASQ'ETS rises and takes the salmon from TH'OWXIYA's belly and begins to dance around the stage. The BOY SPA:TH and the GIRL SPA:TH try to catch the salmon. They go upstage and fall asleep in front of the door-mouth.

Thunder is heard in the distance. SASQ'ETS *returns the salmon to the belly of* TH'OWXIYA.

SQEWEQS *is asleep at the feet of* TH'OWXIYA.

ACTOR 1 *changes the spindle whorl.*

KW'AT'EL WHORL

ACTOR 1: This is the tale
Of how Kw'at'el
Met Sqeweqs

ACTOR 2: That Sqeweqs
Is such a character
He always did make
Me laugh
He sure knows
How to create a good story

ACTOR 1: Quiet now
The first moon has risen and
This is where Kw'at'el
Learns about
The young Spa:th

The Spa:th are sleeping
And when they wake
They will be hungry
They must still
Learn the ways of the earth
And they will learn about the thunder
Quiet now
The story has begun

KW'AT'EL comes scurrying out of his house in a panic.

KW'AT'EL: Th'owxyia has taken my family! The first moon has risen! Ohh no . . . one more moon and all is lost! I must find her some children or else she will eat my family!

KW'AT'EL scurries to the left and then to the right and almost trips over the sleeping SQEWEQS. KW'AT'EL goes up closer to him and begins to sniff SQEWEQS, hoping maybe this is a child. SQEWEQS laughs and this causes KW'AT'EL to scurry a few feet away as SQEWEQS wakes up. Then KW'AT'EL goes back and sniffs again.

SQEWEQS: Hey, cut it out, that tickles. Sniffing me like that, it tickles my feathers. Who are you?

KW'AT'EL: I am Kw'at'el.

SQEWEQS: Wow! You're a real Kw'at'el?

KW'AT'EL: Hey, quit sniffing me!

SQEWEQS: A real Kw'at'el! You sure are small. I always thought Kw'at'el were great big monsters.

SQEWEQS begins to carve a piece of wood.

KW'AT'EL: No, Kw'at'el are small, but I am the biggest of my family. What is that you are carving?

SQEWEQS: This? This is my spoon. I carved it from a tall tree.

KW'AT'EL: It sure is a small spoon . . . but a nice one.

SQEWEQS tries to fit the spoon into his big beak but he can't, so he offers the spoon to KW'AT'EL.

SQEWEQS: Here, you can have the spoon. I will carve myself another.

KW'AT'EL: Thanks?!?

SQEWEQS: Why are you here?

KW'AT'EL: I have travelled many miles and I am on a journey for Th'owxiya.

SQEWEQS: Who's this Thowaxeena?

KW'AT'EL: It's not Thowaxeena, it's Th'owxiya. Th'owxiya is everywhere! She is a Great Spirit! She is a wonderful feast dish where bountiful, delicious foods are prepared and served from.

SQEWEQS: Oh. Does she have any worms? I love big, fat, juicy worms.

KW'AT'EL: She is very powerful!

SQEWEQS: What is this journey that you are on?

KW'AT'EL: I must find and bring to her two young children from the spirit world.

(sotto) You see, she cannot see very well and is very clumsy . . . Years of too much good food have made her fat and lazy.

(louder) BUT *she is still very dangerous*! I must pay back a debt I owe to her before the next moon rises or else my family will be eaten.

SQEWEQS: She can do this? She is so powerful this Th'owxiya?

KW'AT'EL: Yes, her powers are so mighty.

SQEWEQS: I am not afraid of this feast dish. No one tells the Sqeweqs how to eat his worms.

A crash of thunder and laughter.

KW'AT'EL: Oh noooo!

KW'AT'EL chases his tail.

SQEWEQS: Stop!!!
She sounds angry. What was it that you did to displease her?

KW'AT'EL: I borrowed . . . *stole* . . . a piece of cheese from her mouth.

SQEWEQS: So now you must bring her two children and she will forgive you??

KW'AT'EL: She will not eat my family if I bring to her two tasty children for her to dine upon.

SQEWEQS: I will help you. I am not afraid of this dish. She sounds pretty mean, but I am wise and I have fooled many spirits in my time.

KW'AT'EL: Do you know of any children in this spirit world?

SQEWEQS: I know of only two young Spa:th who are sleeping over there . . .

KW'AT'EL: Oh???

SQEWEQS: . . . but they would not be suitable food for a hungry, wild feast dish.

> *KW'AT'EL goes over to the sleeping BOY SPA:TH and GIRL SPA:TH and sniffs them. They are sleeping in front of the door-mouth. Thunder is heard again and is followed by the laughter of* TH'OWXIYA.

KW'AT'EL: *(to audience)* They will make a fine dish for Th'owxiya. She will be pleased with my offering.

(to SQEWEQS) Will you help me carry them to her?

SQEWEQS: No, I will not. They are my friends. We have eaten worms from the same earth. We have flown to the sun! I cannot give them to that wild spirit.

KW'AT'EL: But you said that you would help me. I need these young Spa:th so my family can live.

SQEWEQS: I will help you, but not by sacrificing my young friends. We must think of a way to trick this Th'owxiya.

KW'AT'EL: How can we trick her? I have tried every trick in the book, but she knows all the tricks of the land.

SQEWEQS: She hasn't met the Sqeweqs. I know a few tricks! No one can out trick the Sqeweqs. Come.

SQEWEQS puts his wing around KW'AT'EL and they go and sit beside the sleeping BOY SPA:TH and GIRL SPA:TH. SASQ'ETS begins to move and dance around TH'OWXIYA. Thunder.

SASQ'ETS: That Kw'at'el must bring Th'owxiya the children
There must be children for Th'owxiya to eat
She will not be satisfied
She will not be satisfied

Bring me the children
I will prepare them
She likes them warm
She likes them tasty

Th'owxiya will not be satisfied
She will watch my every move
One more moon
One more moon
There must be children
Or she will turn on me
She will spit fire!
And burn my backside!

I must prepare the other dishes
Th'owxiya is growing old
She cannot see very well
I must move fast
I must stay away from her mouth

> SASQ'ETS *moves very quickly. She continues as thunder and the
> sound of* TH'OWXIYA'S *laughter is heard.* SASQ'ETS *moves about
> and prepares for the feast. She avoids* TH'OWXIYA'S *mouth.*

Such a lovely creature you are
The great Th'owxiya
So wise and magical
So young and beautiful

Look at her lovely mouth
But do not get too close
Her breath is like fire
Look at her lovely arms
But do not get too close
They will hold you forever

Where is that Kw'at'el?
Surely he has found some children
When will he come?

Sqeweqs must not help Kw'at'el
Sqeweqs must not keep the second moon from rising
Sqeweqs must not help Kw'at'el

> *She freezes as* TH'OWXIYA *is heard . . . thunder.*

TH'OWXIYA: Where is my dinner?
Where are those sweet warm children?
Sasq'ets, you have not forgotten, have you?

Remember my breath
Do not forget my wrath
I am the great Th'owxiya!
No one escapes my powers
Bring me the children!

Where is that Kw'at'el?
One more moon
One more moon
OR I will eat his family
A family of Kw'at'el for my belly
One more moon!

> TH'OWXIYA *laughs as* SASQ'ETS *hides.* SQEWEQS *and* KW'AT'EL
> *rise and begin to dance. This causes the* BOY SPA:TH *and the*
> GIRL SPA:TH *to wake. They rise and stretch. They join* SQEWEQS

and KW'AT'EL in their dance. All stop as they hear the laughter and thunder from the voice of TH'OWXIYA.

GIRL SPA:TH: Thunder?

BOY SPA:TH: I think so. Is it, Sqeweqs?

SQEWEQS: Yes . . .

KW'AT'EL: . . . and no. It is thunder, but not real thunder . . . Oh, I am Kw'at'el!

GIRL SPA:TH: What do you mean not real thunder?

KW'AT'EL: That is the voice and laughter of Th'owxiya.

GIRL SPA:TH: Who is Th'owxiya?

KW'AT'EL: Th'owxiya is a Great Spirit *(sotto)* who just loves young Spa:th.

GIRL SPA:TH: Maybe she can help us find our parents.

BOY SPA:TH: Yes, perhaps she is powerful enough to see the whole earth.

KW'AT'EL: She is. You must meet her. She will love to *eat* you! . . . Ahh . . . I mean *meet* you.

SQEWEQS: He means *eat* you. Th'owxiya has a taste for children.

GIRL SPA:TH: She sounds evil.

BOY SPA:TH: Let her try and eat me! I will take care of her with my sharp claws.

> *Thunder is heard, this time much louder and much closer.*
> *TH'OWXIYA begins to laugh.*
>
> *The thunder stops and then the laughter fades.*
>
> *KW'AT'EL starts to chase his own tail. The BOY SPA:TH and the*
> *GIRL SPA:TH think this is a game and start to chase KW'AT'EL's*
> *tail too.*

KW'AT'EL: Stop it! Stop it!

GIRL SPA:TH: Why do you chase your tail?

KW'AT'EL: Because I am nervous!

BOY SPA:TH: Why are you nervous, Kw'at'el?

KW'AT'EL: I am nervous because Th'owxiya is hungry and I must bring her two children or else she will eat my family.

> *KW'AT'EL retreats and stares at his tail and begins to weep. The*
> *GIRL SPA:TH goes up to KW'AT'EL and pulls playfully on his big*
> *whiskers.*

GIRL SPA:TH: Do not cry, Kw'at'el. Perhaps we can help you.

BOY SPA:TH: Yes, perhaps we can trick this Great Spirit.

SQEWEQS walks away and is thinking, then gets a great idea and starts looking for worms. In a small corner of the audience he shows the kids the sleeping worm and whispers to them in secret.

SQEWEQS: Watch me as I trick this Great Spirit—Th'owxiya. I'll gobble up this sleeping worm. Soo juicy.

SQEWEQS gobbles up the worm.

I love to trick spirits! This is a great trick . . . you'll see!

SQEWEQS yawns.

I'm getting soo sleepy . . . I must dream . . .

SQEWEQS falls dead asleep near the kids.

KW'AT'EL: How can we trick her? She is so wise and powerful.

GIRL SPA:TH: We must offer her something more wonderful than children.

KW'AT'EL: What is more wonderful than children to an old hungry spirit?

BOY SPA:TH: What has happened to Sqeweqs?!

The BOY SPA:TH *bends down and picks up a half-eaten worm that was given to him by* SASQ'ETS.

(to kids) What happened to Sqeweqs? Do you know?

KIDS: He ate a sleeping worm! *(or no response)*

GIRL SPA:TH: What's a sleeping worm? *(or I think he ate a sleeping worm!)*

Thunder is heard and is followed by TH'OWXIYA'S *laughter.*

BOY SPA:TH: She is powerful, this Th'owxiya.

GIRL SPA:TH: Poor Sqeweqs.

KW'AT'EL: *(running)* We must hide. She will come for us if we stay here by Sqeweqs.

BOY SPA:TH: Where shall we go?

KW'AT'EL: Sqeweqs must sleep off the power of that sleeping worm. We must leave!

GIRL SPA:TH: Will Th'owxiya eat Sqeweqs?

KW'AT'EL: Yes . . . No! . . . She doesn't care much for Sqeweqs. He will be all right. Come, we must leave. Help me save my family before it's too late!

BOY SPA:TH: We must save our friend!

KW'AT'EL: Ohhh . . . You're right.

BOY SPA:TH: What smells funny?

KW'AT'EL: Sorry about that. Too much cheese.

KW'AT'EL waves his tail.

Thunder is heard.

TH'OWXIYA: Kw'at'el, you are too late! Your family is being prepared right this minute. Umm, how tasty they shall be. My servant is buttering them up right now.

Once the second moon rises behind the great mountain, I shall have your family for dinner! Unless you give me some nice warm children.

TH'OWXIYA laughs and thunder crashes all around and then both fade away.

A puppet of SQEWEQS rises from behind the set. Dreamy music plays.

KW'AT'EL: Wait! Sqeweqs is helping us!

BOY SPA:TH & GIRL SPA:TH: What?!!?

KW'AT'EL: Look! He's tricking Th'owxiya! He *can* keep the second moon from rising!

A puppet show of clouds, moon, sun and SQEWEQS plays.

RAVEN WHORL

SASQ'ETS: We are in Sqeweqs's dream

ALL: We are what he sees right now

BOY SPA:TH & GIRL SPA:TH: The clouds

KW'AT'EL: The moon

ALL: Sqeweqs dreams of flying
He dreams of flying to the moon

GIRL SPA:TH: I am a white cloud
I hold no rain
I am a cloud for a sunny day

BOY SPA:TH: I am a rain cloud
I hold all the rain
I am a cloud for a rainy day

KW'AT'EL: I am the moon
I hold all the light
I am the moon and I am *cool*

KW'AT'EL: Look at silly Sqeweqs
Look how he chases me
Look how he chases the moon

BOY SPA:TH: Look at funny Sqeweqs
Look at how he flaps his wings
Look at him sleep

GIRL SPA:TH: Look at Sqeweqs
Look at his tired wings

Let us help Sqeweqs
Flap your wings!
Poor Sqeweqs is still asleep

KW'AT'EL: He is trying to steal me
He is trying to take the light
The Sqeweqs is trying to steal the moon

SASQ'ETS: This is only a dream

GIRL SPA:TH: The sun is not out
The Sqeweqs dreams of the moon

SASQ'ETS: This is only a dream

GIRL SPA:TH: The Sqeweqs is sound asleep
Look at the way he flaps his wings

BOY SPA:TH: He's getting stronger
He's getting close to the moon!
He's keeping the moon from rising!

> *The BOY SPA:TH and the GIRL SPA:TH follow SQEWEQS and then slowly lead the puppet out. They disappear but the two SQEWEQSES are joined together and they sink behind the set wall.*

STORYTELLING

ACTOR 1: Sqeweqs is a very tricky spirit
He has kept the second moon from rising

ACTOR 2: He must wake
And fly to the night
And bring light
To the dark earth

ACTOR 1: But first he must help
The young Spa:th
And that poor Kw'at'el

ACTOR 2: I sure hope that
Mean old Th'owxiya
Gets what's coming to her

ACTOR 1: We shall see
We shall see . . .

KWAT'EL exits.

SASQ'ETS rises and looks about at the night. She is searching for the moon. She checks TH'OWXIYA's mouth to see if she has eaten it. Thunder is heard and this causes SASQ'ETS to jump back and continue with her work, but then starts to exit. SASQ'ETS freezes as the BOY SPA:TH and the GIRL SPA:TH enter.

BOY SPA:TH & GIRL SPA:TH: Where is Kw'at'el?

SQEWEQS: He is gone to the great mountain. The mountain is telling him how to appease Th'owxiya.

BOY SPA:TH: We must go to the great mountain!

SQEWEQS: Yes! And listen and learn the song that you will need to please Th'owxiya.

GIRL SPA:TH: Yes.

SQEWEQS: The great mountain is where the magic song is that you need to sing for Th'owxiya.

BOY SPA:TH: Come, we must go to the great mountain. There we will learn how to soothe Th'owxiya.

SASQ'ETS enters and sees that the moon has not risen yet. She begins to dust TH'OWXIYA as she speaks.

FEAST

SASQ'ETS: The second moon has not risen!

You are powerful, Th'owxiya
You are the most powerful feast dish on earth

Let us dust you off
For the feast shall soon be starting

Nice warm Kw'at'el
Nice tasty Kw'at'el for dinner

The sauce is almost ready
One more stir of the spoon

Where is the spoon?
Have I forgotten the spoon?

Yes, I have forgotten it
Did I bring the water?

Where is the water?
I have forgotten that, too!
Where is the water?

It's probably with the spoon
Which I forgot?
Why can I not remember anything?

Quiet, Th'owxiya will hear me
Quiet . . .

> *TH'OWXIYA laughs and yawns as she wakes up. SASQ'ETS pretends to be mixing the sauce and pouring the water.*

TH'OWXIYA: Why is the sauce not prepared?
Have you not stirred the sauce?
Where is the spoon?

SASQ'ETS: I forgot it
It was my fault!

TH'OWXIYA: FOOL! Bring me a drink of water. My lips are dry and my throat needs sweet water. Where is the water?

SASQ'ETS: I forgot it too!
It was my fault!

TH'OWXIYA: How can I eat without a spoon and a cool drink of sweet water?! You fool, you shall pay for this! Where is that Kw'at'el? Where is the second moon? Once it rises above the great mountain and touches the night I will eat him, his family, and then I will have you for dessert.

> *TH'OWXIYA laughs as thunder comes crashing down. SASQ'ETS runs and hides as the thunder and laughter fade. She stands as KW'AT'EL comes scurrying out of the house. KW'AT'EL is carrying a rainbow fabric and stands near TH'OWXIYA as SQEWEQS begins to flap his wings amongst the audience: CAA CAA.*

KW'AT'EL: I could not find any children. I only could find two young Spa:th and now they are my friends. The great mountain gave me this rainbow and I have brought it to trade for my family. I do not believe that Th'owxiya has a rainbow, does she?

> *The long fabric is pulled out for the front rows of the audience in an arc. Drumbeat music starts.*

SASQ'ETS: Th'owxiya is ready to eat your family
She will eat them
Yes, eat them when the second moon has risen

KW'AT'EL: But surely she will want a rainbow. It will help her see better and maybe she wouldn't be so angry. Isn't that what you want, Sasq'ets?

SASQ'ETS: You have a point
What else could you offer?

KW'AT'EL: I have this spoon . . .

SQEWEQS: CAA

KW'AT'EL: . . . that Sqeweqs gave to me.

SASQ'ETS: I need a spoon
Without it, I will be dessert
What else?

The BOY SPA:TH runs in. The drumbeat gets stronger.

BOY SPA:TH: I have a bowl of sweet, cool water given to me by the great mountain so I can cleanse my spirit. The mountain told me that my parents have become great trees in the spirit world and that they are watching over me. I give Th'owxiya this bowl of sweet water so Kw'at'el can watch over his family.

SASQ'ETS: This is good
Th'owxiya wants a drink of sweet water
What else do you have?

The GIRL SPA:TH runs in. The drumbeat gets stronger.

GIRL SPA:TH: I have a rattle given to me by the great mountain. The mountain said that my parents are watching over me and this rattle will help me dream of them at night. You may use it on Th'owxiya so Kw'at'el can watch over his family.

SASQ'ETS: The rattle is good
She will like the rattle
Yes, the rattle is good

Maybe she will not eat Kw'at'el's family!
This is good!

KW'AT'EL: Th'owxiya! Please accept these gifts! I do not want my family to be eaten!

SASQ'ETS: I will try and please her with your gifts
I will take these gifts and I will try
I will try to appease Th'owxiya

> *Thunder rolls . . . SASQ'ETS begins her ceremony. SQEWEQS goes to the sun puppet. SASQ'ETS shakes the rattle. Everyone starts to sing the "Celebration Song."*
>
> *SASQ'ETS shakes the rattle and moves around the rainbow and all the gifts. SQEWEQS goes behind the wall as the sun rises. The thunder ends.*
>
> *TH'OWXIYA speaks in a softer, more loving voice.*

TH'OWXIYA: Sasq'ets, why is the sun out? Why didn't the second moon rise? Why is my belly full? Ummm . . . delicious sweet, cool water! Where is Kw'at'el? Have I already eaten him? Have I eaten his family?? Where did that rainbow come from? Sasq'ets, you are the best, always taking care of me. I will not eat you, or you and your family, Kw'at'el. Let us have a feast. Please come and be happy! Help yourselves. There is enough to share!

KW'AT'EL: Do you have any cheese?

SQEWEQS: Do you have any worms?

BOY SPA:TH & GIRL SPA:TH: Do you have any salmon?

TH'OWXIYA: Yes, I have everything!
Come and join us in the celebration!

SASQ'ETS: We have plenty for everyone
Come and eat her foods!

GIRL SPA:TH: Come and join us in our song to Th'owxiya

> *SASQ'ETS shakes the rattle. All sing the new song from the mountain.*

FEAST SONG

ALL: Hey O O
Hey O O
Hey O O ah hey

Hey O O
Hey O O
Hey O O ah hey

STORYTELLING FINALE

ACTOR 1: That was a good tale
Everyone is happy
Everyone has a full belly

ACTOR 2: Th'owxiya is happy
And her belly
Is full for another day
And now she can sleep

ACTOR 4: We shall put
The spindle away
For now

ACTOR 5: But do come back
And we will spin
Another world for
The spirits to dance within

ACTOR 3: Come back
And we will tell you
Another story

VOICE OF TH'OWXIYA: See you
My friends

The song rises into a canon as the storytellers encourage the audience on stage to dance.

End.

STUDY GUIDE

This study guide includes suggestions about preparing your students to interact with the text in order to help them take more from their reading experience. Included is information and ideas on how to use the book to enhance aspects of your education curriculum, with exercises that respond to the themes and dramatic elements presented in the play.

1. SYNOPSIS

Indigenous storytellers spin the Kwantlen First Nations tale of
Th'owxiya: The Hungry Feast Dish. The mouth of Th'owxiya holds
the most wonderful foods from around the world. However, if
you steal from her, you will pay a terrible price, for Th'owxiya has
developed a taste for children! When a brave young Kw'at'el (mouse)
takes a piece of cheese from Th'owxiya, he is caught. To appease the
ogress, he must find two young spirits to sacrifice to her before the
second moon rises or she will eat his whole family! With the help
of two Spa:th (bears), a Sqeweqs (raven) and a Sasq'ets (sasquatch),
Kw'at'el sets forth on a journey for knowledge and forgiveness.
Th'owxiya: The Hungry Feast Dish has shades of "Hansel and Gretel"
and the First Nations story "The Wild Woman of the Woods," told
through mask and music.

ORIGINS OF THE STORY

Th'owxiya is a scary spirit. Some say she is a giant. She has great powers. Elders would tell children that if they did not listen and behave she would take them into the forest and eat them. Although she is scary, she also has the power to bring good luck to anyone who has seen her. Because she cannot see very well, she can be easily avoided. She is also said to be rather drowsy and dim-witted. For Kwantlen people, she is a mythological being used to teach children to listen and to not venture off alone or else they may be taken by her.

2. SUPPORTING STORIES

"A LITTLE FISH" BY JOSEPH A. DANDURAND

April
and seagulls swarming up river
to feast on a little fish as we Indians
shake a net loaded with little fish
and we catch five hundred pounds
and we put them away to burn later
in the year for our dead
our loved ones
our past

this little fish used to be in the millions
and we used to be able to scoop them up
and feast on them
but like all fools of our people all we
get now are small tastes of this little fish
because the world today loves
to wipe out food of our past
but
Indians
are still here and like

the little fish
we have somehow survived

as we place the plate of fresh little fish
the fire begins its magic
and the plate of little fish burns
and the smoke goes up
into the sky as the dead and loved
can be heard over the cry
of a thousand seagulls:
thank you

"TWO" BY JOSEPH A. DANDURAND

2 eagles talk
as we track a song
lost in eroded island
bluffs.

2 old drummers
reminisce about what
it used to be like.

fish jumps looks
around
devours the current
and is away.

2 cats lay in dirt
sleepy eyes barely open
dead mouse beside them
not telling tales of last
night's torture.

unknown truck
goes by our house
not supposed to be here
strangers
in a strange land.

old reserve #6
an island
squa'lets
its old name.
(where waters divide)

2 indian kids play hockey
one shoots
one saves
they are not strangers
nor is this place strange to
them.

old rez #6
an island that
becomes more
of an island
less of an island.

eroded
by the
fraser river.

squa'lets

this old place
not a strange
word anymore.

language is like that:

taken
eroded

returned.

THE WILD WOMAN OF THE WOODS

The Northwest Coast First Nations all tell the tales of the Wild Woman of the Woods.

A fearsome figure supposedly twice as big as regular humans, the Wild Woman is a basket ogress with great powers. Elders would tell children that if they foolishly ventured into the forest alone, the Wild Woman would capture them, put them into the great basket on her back and whisk them back to her cave to be eaten.

Although the Wild Woman is a warning to naughty children to stay out of the dark and dangerous parts of the forest, she is also a bringer of great fortune—bestowing wealth to any who are able to outwit or control her.

The basket ogress is thought to have limited eyesight and is often depicted as drowsy or dim-witted.

Other names for the Wild Woman of the Woods include Tsonokwa, Dzonokwa, Zuniquwa, Wealth Giver, Giantess, Th'owxiya, Basket Ogress.

The following is one of her many stories.

The children of the village played at the edge of a great forest. One girl was very small, and was often teased by the other children. She knew that they shouldn't play in the forest for the elders had told them to beware of the giant women that lived deep in the woods. But children are curious creatures and soon they were farther into the forest than they should have been.

From behind a rock, the ogress appeared, her giant basket held on her back. She scooped the naughty children into her basket, singing, "I will have a great feast tonight" and took them back to her cave.

The children struggled in the basket, but there was nothing that they could do. The lid of the basket was strong. There was no way out except for a small hole in the bottom where the basket was frayed. The children tried to get through the hole, but it was too small. Finally they let the smallest girl try and she easily slipped through the hole and fell to the ground. She ran as fast as she could back to the village where she told the elders what had happened.

The people from the village followed the basket ogress up into the mountains to her cave where her servant was preparing a fire to cook the captive children. All the while the ogress danced and sang, "The children will be roasted, I will have a great feast tonight!" The people of the village hid in the trees until the fire was burning hot and the ogress was drowsy from dancing and they sang a song that put the drowsy creature to sleep. She stumbled, knocking over her basket, and fell into the fire where she burned.

The children never questioned the elders and never wandered too far into the forest again.

HANSEL AND GRETEL (GRIMMS' FAIRY TALE)

Next to the forest lived a poor woodcutter, his two children—Hansel and Gretel—and his new wife. They were very poor and when famine came to the land, the woodcutter could no longer provide their daily bread.

The stepmother, who was selfish and had no love for the children, came up with a plan to leave them in the woods to starve. Hansel and Gretel overheard this and made a plan of their own. Their stepmother led them into the woods and left them there, but Hansel and Gretel had left a trail of pebbles behind and easily found their way back.

The stepmother convinced the father to try her plan again, this time preventing the children from collecting pebbles to make a trail. The second time they were led into the woods, the children tried to leave a trail of bread crumbs, but the crumbs were eaten by birds. They were lost.

As they wandered hungry and alone in the woods, they came across the most amazing house they had ever seen, with walls of bread, a roof of cake and windows made of clear sugar! The children began to eat from the house when they hear a soft voice saying, "Nibble, nibble, little mouse, who is nibbling at my house?"

An old woman stood in the doorway. She was blind and had a long, pointed nose. She invited the children inside and gave them warm pancakes with mild sugar, apples and nuts. That night, while the children were sleeping peacefully, she snatched Hansel from the bed and put him in a cage. Then she woke Gretel roughly and forced her to cook and clean for her. "When your brother is plump, I will eat him for supper!" The witch forced Gretel to cook all the best foods for Hansel and then she would go to the cage and order him to stick out his finger so she could see if he was plump. Hansel stuck out a small bone instead, but the witch was blind, so she felt the bone and wondered why Hansel wasn't getting plump.

Eventually the witch got tired of waiting and instructed Gretel to stoke the fire in the oven and prepare water so that she could cook and eat Hansel. When the fire was stoked, she told Gretel to climb into the oven to check if the fire was ready to bake. She meant to trick Gretel so she could lock her in the oven and bake her too!

Gretel was too clever for her trick, saying, "The oven is too small, I won't fit inside."

The witch, who was very hungry and not very smart said, "Stupid goose. The opening is big enough. See, I myself could get in," and stuck her head into the oven.

Gretel pushed as hard as she could. The witch toppled headfirst into the oven and Gretel slammed the door behind her.

Gretel let her brother out of the cage and together they began the journey home, stuffing their pockets with treasures from the witch's house as they left.

When they arrived at home, they found their father alone and very sad. Their stepmother had died and their father had tried for many days to search the woods for his children. With the treasure they had taken from the witch, the family lived happily ever after.

3. Q&A WITH PLAYWRIGHT JOSEPH A. DANDURAND

WHAT DOES THIS STORY MEAN TO YOU?

I have to think back to when I actually wrote this piece twenty-five years ago. I was an intern in a pilot program for Aboriginals to study museology at the new Museum of Civilization in Ottawa. My internship included working with the in-house interpretative theatre company. I would spend days in the Grand Hall, where I first met the feast dish Th'owxiya. For me, this story shows the beginnings of a playwright. I was just out of theatre school and had only written a few plays at that point. This story took on a life of its own as I began to explore the many spirits and characters that come from our people. This story is a gift and will hopefully carry on as a story for generations to come.

WHAT IS YOUR BACKGROUND?

My father was white and my mother is from Kwantlen. I am also a registered member of the Nooksack people located just across the border. My grandfather was Nooksack. I am and have always believed that I am Kwantlen. As for my educational background, I have studied at Algonquin College and went to the University of

Ottawa, where I studied acting and direction. As far as my writing, I am self-taught and have been writing plays and poetry for the past twenty-five years.

TELL US ABOUT THE TRADITIONS OF MUSIC AND STORY-TELLING IN FIRST NATIONS CULTURE.

Our traditions, ceremonies and rituals have been here since we began as a people. The use of both story and music can be found in any ceremony that we perform. There is not one without the other. Even the simple sharing of a meal will include a dinner song to bless the food.

TELL US ABOUT THE CHARACTERS IN THE PLAY.

The characters in this play are ones that I use throughout my work. In both my plays and my poetry, I constantly use spiritual beings. I write a lot about the raven and the wolf but also about being a fisherman. The river and the fish are very prevalent in my work. Most of my plays are set on or near a river. I think the fact that I live on an island has a lot to do with that. The use of characters has many elements. For example, Sasq'ets. We can get away from what folks think of sasquatch being this creature that stays hidden from us by giving Sasq'ets more human feelings and needs. Also, the feast dish comes alive even though she is a feast dish. I believe that children will learn from this story to welcome animal spirits into their everyday.

TELL US ABOUT THE SETTING IN THE PLAY.

The story is set in a simple Kwantlen village. With our traditional longhouses there is a single door for each family, but in this tale, the doorways are for the spirits. Kwantlen spirits, though some live inside, are mostly found outdoors: along the river, on top of a mountain, in the sky or simply in the open where a feast dish lives.

4. CONNECTIONS

THEMES

» Respecting the environment
» Problem-solving and friendship
» Courage, co-operation and honour
» Mask, puppets, music and songs as forms of communication

ARTS EDUCATION CURRICULUM CONNECTION K–7

» Drama Curriculum (responding to, reflecting on and analyzing drama presentations).

» people create art to express who they are as individuals and as a community
» dance, drama, music and visual arts are each unique languages for creating and communicating
» people connect to the hearts and minds of others in a variety of places and times through the arts
» experiencing art challenges our point of view and expands our understanding of others

» Music Curriculum (responding to, reflecting on and analyzing music performances).

  » music is created and performed within a wide range of historical, cultural and social contexts

» Literary Curriculum (recognize advanced vocabulary, analyze oral language and communication strategies, read and demonstrate comprehension).

  » exploring stories and other texts help us understand ourselves and make connections to others and to the world
  » everyone has a unique story to share

SOCIAL RESPONSIBILITY CONNECTION K–7

» The themes in the play support an understanding of the importance of contributing to community, solving problems in a peaceful way, defending human rights and exercising democratic rights and responsibilities.

FIRST PEOPLES' PRINCIPLES OF LEARNING

» *Th'owxiya* incorporates the following First Peoples' Principles of Learning:

> » learning ultimately supports the well-being of the self, the family, the community, the land, the spirits and the ancestors
> » learning is holistic, reflexive, reflective, experiential and relational (focused on connectedness, reciprocal relationships and a sense of place)
> » learning involves recognizing the consequences of one's actions
> » learning involves generational roles and responsibilities
> » learning recognizes the role of Indigenous knowledge
> » learning is embedded in memory, history and story
> » learning involves patience and time
> » learning requires exploration of one's identity
> » learning involves recognizing that some knowledge is sacred and only shared with permission and / or in certain situations

The First Peoples' Principles of Learning provided by First Nations Education Steering Committee (www.fnesc.ca).

5. ACTIVITIES

REVIEWING TH'OWXYIA: THE HUNGRY FEAST DISH

Now that your students have read *Th'owxiya: The Hungry Feast Dish*, it is the perfect time to expand on their excitement and interest in drama and music and to discuss ideas and themes presented in the book.

The following questions can be used for group discussions or for sharing with a partner or in a small group. After sharing with a partner or small group, students can take turns sharing ideas with the whole group.

If using the questions as sentence starters for a writing activity, the students can also draw pictures to accompany their writing.

» Who was your favourite character? Why?
» What character would you like to have as a friend? Why?
» What character would you not want to have as a friend? Why?
» If you could be an actor in *Th'owxiya*, which character would you like to be? Why?
» What do you think it takes to be a good actor or musician?
» What was the scariest part of the play? Why?
» What was the funniest part of the play? Why?
» What part of the play surprised you the most? Why?

» If you were the playwright, what would happen next in *Th'owxiya*?

» The Spa:th and Sqeweqs work hard to help their friend Kw'at'el. Which friends have you helped in difficult times? What did you do to help them?

» The original production involved the use of masks and intricate costumes. How would you use costumes and masks make your own version of the play?

There are a variety of ways for students to respond to, reflect on and analyze drama and musical performances: for example, through talking, writing, stories, art, singing and playing drama games. The following suggestions will help to engage your students in activities where fun and laughter are often as important as building skills to increase critical thinking, self-awareness and confidence. Choose the activities that are best suited to your grade level and, if necessary, modify the skill level of the activities to meet the needs of your students.

DISCUSS THE THEME OF RESPECT FOR THE ENVIRONMENT

In *Th'owxiya*, Sqeweqs (the raven) talked about the earth: "Should we eat the earth? Yes, but we must not eat too much. We must save some for the next generation. Remember that, do not eat too much of the earth. Save some."

Why do we want to save the earth for other generations? David Suzuki works very hard to educate people on the environment and climate change, please visit his website for more information on what you can do to help, http://www.davidsuzuki.org/take-action/

PLAYING WITH SONG AND STORY

Using a familiar song that the students love to sing, write a class story related to the song. Add characters, simple dialogue and actions that can help to make the song come alive! By combining the story and the song, the students will experience the fun of participating in a musical drama. Challenge the students to vary the tone of their voices and to use body movements to help portray the personalities of the characters in the story. Experiment with using simple sound effects, props and costumes.

MASKS AND PUPPETS

Children love the magic and intrigue associated with masks and puppets. Although creating your own masks and puppets in the classroom requires extra time and effort, the result will most certainly outweigh all other considerations. The use of masks and puppets will enhance the enjoyment and deepen the understanding of many classroom activities related to drama, storytelling, music, singing, body movement and art.

GEOGRAPHY

Make a colourful map of the different First Nations territories in your area. Discuss how these regions intersect with other cities and towns in the area.

HAVE FUN WITH DRAMA GAMES: PANTOMIME

A great way to start playing with drama is with simple pantomimes. Explain to your students that acting is showing. By NOT using words during a pantomime, they become forced to show, not tell.

Copy the list of animals, also translated into the Kwantlen language (found in the Appendix), and cut them out. Have students draw an animal, by themselves or with a partner, and take turns acting like their chosen animal. Encourage the students to exaggerate their body movements in order to help their classmates guess the animal they are portraying.

The students may also be encouraged to come up with their own ideas for pantomimes. Get them started with these suggestions: tying a shoe, brushing their teeth, eating spaghetti, riding on a skateboard, playing basketball or painting a mural.

HAVE FUN WITH DRAMA GAMES: MIRRORS

A game of mirrors is a great group activity that gets students working together and paying close attention to each other. Have the students pair off in A/B partners around the classroom. To begin, A will be the actor and B the mirror. The two partners face each other and while partner A begins to move, partner B will mirror everything that partner A does. When you call out "freeze," partner B will become the actor and partner A will be the mirror. Do this a few times throughout the activity.

HAVE FUN WITH DRAMA GAMES: WHAT ARE YOU DOING?

In a circle, one person in the centre performs an activity until someone jumps in and asks, "What are you doing?" The person in the centre says something different from what they are doing and the person who jumped in does that new activity.

For example, the person in middle is cutting the lawn, and when another person jumps in and asks, "What are you doing?" the person in middle says, "Screwing in a light bulb." The person who jumped in then does that activity . . . and so on around the circle.

RESEARCHING AND REFLECTING ON FIRST NATIONS CULTURE

Suggested questions for K–4 audiences

1. What do you already know about First Nations people?
2. What is a reserve? Why do many First Nations people live on a reserve?
3. Who are Elders? Why are they important?
4. What First Nations stories or songs do you know?
5. What examples of dance, drama, music and visual arts in Indigenous cultures have you seen, heard or do you know about?
6. Which ancestral First Nations territory is your school built on?

Suggested questions for grade 5–7 audiences

1. What assumptions do people make about First Nations people (e.g., they only live in rural areas)?
2. What are some of the challenges faced by Indigenous people in Canada (e.g. poverty)?
3. Why do some First Nations people not live on reserves and why have they left (e.g., schooling, living conditions, etc.)?
4. Who are the Métis people? Who are the Inuit people?
5. Can you think of a famous Indigenous artist, songwriter, actor or performer?

Teacher Note: You may want to reference Buffy Sainte-Marie, Chief Dan George, Corrine Hunt, Graham Greene, Bill Reid, Tomson Highway, or Rita Joe.

Ask individual students or small groups of students to focus on the following components of the play

Setting

» What did the students notice in the setting (e.g., the spindle whorl, the plank house, the door-mouth, etc.)?
» How did the characters interact with their surroundings?
» What were the different places that the characters visited (e.g., the spirit world, the great mountains)?

Music

1. In a circle, have students share, one at a time, appropriate body sound possibilities. For example:

   » suggest an environment and have students each create and share a sound found in it (e.g., the forest, the river, the ocean)
   » discuss and experiment with changing dynamics, volume, tempo, colour

2. In the play, there are several locations described that inspire sound. Give small groups of students one of the following locations or situations from the play and ask them to create a soundscape:

   » a peaceful mountainous windy outdoor location
   » inside Sqeweqs's dream
   » high above the great mountains
   » running in the forest
   » the spirit world
   » hiding from Th'owxiya
   » Th'owxiya's thunderous laughter

The Drum

In a circle, do a shared reading of the following information about drums:

» In the Kwantlen Nation, drumming is a very important part of the tradition and culture. To the Kwantlen people, drumming brings down the spirit of the occasion.

» The drum is a very important part of First Nations music.

» The drum is the beat that all the dancers move to.

» Some people say that the drum makes the sound of a heartbeat.

» In a way, the drum is the heart of the powwow.

» The host drum is usually made up of a group of eight men.

» They sit around a very large drum that is about one and a half metres in diameter.

» The drum is made out of deer-, elk-, buffalo- or cowhide, and each person has a leather mallet that they beat in unison on the drum.

» Each powwow has a host drum, and usually several guest drums.

» Men are the traditional drummers at powwows, but women often take part by singing the songs with the drummers. It would be pretty hard to have a powwow without a drum.

» Powwow songs are usually sung in the traditional language of the drummers.

» Some songs are centuries old, while others were written more recently.

» There are also songs that use sounds, called vocables, instead of words.

» The drummers sing sounds like "Ah Hey Yah Ho," which makes it possible for everyone to join in.

6. PACIFIC NORTHWEST FIRST NATIONS

The Kwantlen (Qw'?ntl'en) Nation (http://www.kwantlenfn.ca/) are part of the Stó:lō Nation and inhabit the river around the Fraser Valley. Since time immemorial, they live by the seven traditional laws that guided their ancestors: health, happiness, generations, generosity, humbleness, forgiveness and understanding. Through learning, family, health, their culture and traditions and looking after their lands and resources, they are tireless in their spirit to make a better world for their future generations. In working together and learning from their Elders, they are respectful, proud, independent and responsible.

The Stó:lō Nation (http://www.sfu.museum/time/en/panoramas/beach/culture/) are the original inhabitants of the Fraser Valley; they have been there since time immemorial and continue to live there today. The villages along the Fraser River housed hundreds of people in large structures called longhouses that have stood for hundreds of years in one location passed down from one generation to the next. Prior to initial contact with European newcomers, the Stó:lō population was estimated to number up to thirty thousand people.

The Musqueam (xʷməθkʷəy̓əm) Nation (http://www.musqueam
.bc.ca/) have lived in their present location for thousands of years.
Their traditional territory occupies what is now Vancouver and its
surrounding areas. The name Musqueam relates back to the River
Grass, məθkʷəy̓. There is a story that has been passed on from generation to generation that explains how they became known as the
xʷməθkʷəy̓əm, People of the River Grass.

KWANTLEN FIRST NATION HISTORY

The Kwantlen First Nation were recorded in 1827 as the largest
group on the lower Fraser, with a traditional territory extending
from Mud Bay in Tsawwassen, through the Serpentine and Salmon
Rivers and along the Fraser River, east past Mission. Kwantlen
is a hun'qumi'num word meaning "tireless hunters" or "tireless
runners."

The Kwantlen are Stó:lō people, or "river people" who depend
upon the river and land for their survival and livelihood. The Stó:lō
share a common language known a Halkomelem (Halq'eméylem),
of the Coast Salish language family.

Elders explain how Xá:ls (the Creator), placed the Kwantlen
people under the shores of the Fraser River so they would have
access to the area's rich resources. The legend tells of the first
Kwantlen named "Swaniset," meaning to come or appear in a mys-
terious manner, was a "Ten Sweyil," or a descendent of the sky, who
suddenly appeared on the river. Xá:ls gave Swaniset all the tools and
knowledge he would need to become a great hunter and fisherman,
as well as a great leader. Under Swaniset and his successors the
Kwantlen people thrived for countless generations.

Salmon was the primary resource of the Kwantlen people, was the basis of their economy and held sacred as a gift from Xá:ls. The salmon runs determined the seasonal cycle of the Kwantlen people, who joined many other Nations in their summer homes on the tributaries and lakes to fish and preserve, by either smoking or wind drying the salmon for winter. There were reportedly upwards of five thousand First Nations people who gathered in the Kwantlen territory to fish and trade. This peaceful economic trade between the Nations allowed for a rich cultural interchange and preserved cultural unity.

7. APPENDIX

VOCABULARY

Th'owxiya: The feast dish. Th'owxiya is a great and powerful female spirit who is said to eat children. She also doesn't see that well and can be easily fooled.

Sasq'ets: Sasquatch. Sasquatch was a powerful but generally benign supernatural creature in the shape of a very large, hairy wild being. Kwantlen people consider spotting a sasquatch good luck. There's an even better endowment—a golden gift—if the sasquatch sees you.

Kw'at'el: Mouse. A small rodent with a large family.

Sqeweqs: Raven. A large black bird known to be a trickster in the Kwantlen culture.

Theqa:t: Tree.

Spa:th: Bear.

Sp'oq'es: Eagle.

Chitmexw: Owl.

Qw'o':ntl'an: Kwantlen. A First Nations village on the Fraser River, upriver of Musqueam.

Syuwe: Storyteller.

Squa'lets: Translates to "Where Waters Divide," a Kwantlen village.

Celebration Song: A traditional song accompanied by drumming to mark a celebration in the community.

Welcoming Song: A message that can indicate that you are welcome into the village.

Plank House: A traditional West Coast First Nations style of house built with wooden planks.

Longhouses: Usually built from cedar, a wooden-log style building for communal gatherings in Pacific Northwest First Nations.

Door-Mouth: The opening or door at the front of a traditional plank house.

Totem: A totem is a way that First Nations people depict the stories of their family and their culture through carvings. One example of this is the Totem Pole, prevalent in Coast Salish First Nations.

Basket Ogress: Another name for the Wild Woman of the Woods, the spirit woman in Coast Salish folklore.

Feast Dish: A large, carved dish made for celebrations or ceremonies to hold gifts for the community.

Cannibal: A being who eats the flesh or organs of another member of its species.

Sacrifice: To give up (something important or valued) for the sake of other considerations.

Debt: Something owed or due from someone to someone else.

Spindle Whorl: A disc fitted onto a spindle (long stick) to increase and maintain the speed of the spin. Used to make fleece into yarn.

Spirit World: An imaginary world beyond our own full of spirits and magic.

Sleeping Worm: A worm in the spirit world that causes an instant and deep sleep when eaten.

Sweet Berries: Huckleberries, a berry native to the West Coast used as food and traditional medicine by First Nations peoples of the Pacific Northwest and Interior BC.

PANTOMIME SUGGESTIONS

Deer (Tl'elqtele)
Mouse (Kw'at'el)
Rabbit (Shxwoxw)
Frog (Wexes)
Salmon (Stheqi)
Beaver (Sqela:w)
Raven (Sqeweqs)
Wolf (Steqo:ya)
Bear (Spa:th)
Owl (Chitmexw)
Porcupine (Swetiya)
Chipmunk (Xep'i:tsel)
Sasquatch (Sasq'ets)
Moose (Q'oyi:ts)

WEBSITES FOR REFERENCE

The Museum of Anthropology at UBC, http://moa.ubc.ca/

UBC Botanical Garden, http://botanicalgarden.ubc.ca

David Suzuki Foundation, www.davidsuzuki.org

Indigenous Tourism BC, www.indigenousbc.com/

Native Drums, an exciting and innovative website devoted to the rich heritage of First Nations Culture and Music, www.nativedrums.ca

An Indigenous-owned clearinghouse for resources, books, videos, CD ROMs, etc., respectful of First Nations, Métis and Inuit people, their history and culture, http://www.goodminds.com/

Canadian Indigenous Books for schools, http://books.bc.ca /resources/for-librarians-and-educators/

First Voices, a website to help with pronunciation in the Kwantlen Language. www.firstvoices.com

ACKNOWLEDGEMENTS

I would like to thank Axis Theatre for believing in this story and making it better. To all the actors and designers who have worked on this show, I am forever grateful. To the Kwantlen people, my family and friends, I thank you for calling me a storyteller. To the river people, I say thank you for surviving so today I can continue to tell our stories.

Joseph A. Dandurand is a member of Kwantlen First Nation located on the Fraser River east of Vancouver. He resides there with his three children, Danessa, Marlysse and Jace. Joseph is Director of the Kwantlen Cultural Centre, received a diploma in Performing Arts from Algonquin College and studied Theatre and Direction at the University of Ottawa. He is currently the storyteller-in-residence of the Vancouver Public Library. He has published twelve books of poetry, the most recent being *I Want* (Leaf Press), *Hear and Foretell, The Rumour* (BookLand Press) and *Sh:lam (The Doctor)* (Mawenzi House).